Interfaith Dialogue

The teaching of the Catholic Church

Committee for Other Faiths
Catholic Bishops' Conference of England and Wales

Interfaith Dialogue
The teaching of the Catholic Church

Compiled by Alfred Agius for the Committee for Other Faiths
of the Catholic Bishops' Conference of England and Wales

Further information may be obtained from
Committee for Other Faiths, Catholic Bishops' Conference of England
and Wales, 39 Eccleston Square, London SW1V 1BX; tel 020 7901 4841
Westminster Interfaith, 23 Kensington Square, London W8 5HN;
tel 020 7361 4740

Cover picture: Interreligious Assembly, Rome, 28 October 1999
(*L'Osservatore Romano*)

www.catholic-ew.org.uk

Published in February 2002 by the Catholic Communications Service,
39 Eccleston Square, London SW1V 1BX. ccs@cbcew.org.uk

Printed by Hastings Printing Company Ltd, St Leonards-on-Sea

ISBN 0 905241 22 3

Contents

Foreword

It has been said that the world changed on 11 September 2001. The tragic events of that day have spawned a great deal of thought and heart-searching about various issues: about the maintenance of peace in the present world order; about the conflict between the Islamic world and the west; about the significance of religion in human affairs. Clearly there are those who see religion as the root of the problem and would argue that many racial and ethnic conflicts are caused or, at least, exacerbated by religion. In the media there are those who argue that the 'overcoming' of religion would create a better world order. It is significant that their target is normally Christianity, as if western culture, having abandoned its religious roots and origins, is showing the way forward for the human race as a whole.

For several hundred years now, voices in Europe have been heralding the end of religion. But religion has not gone away. It does not go away. Moreover, the events of 11 September have put increasingly before the world the central issue that faces the world today: the relationships between the religions of the world. The question of the coexistence of religions is one that can no longer be evaded. Our security and our future are intimately bound up with this matter.

For this reason the present small volume is very timely. The Second Vatican Council saw the beginning of a whole new body of Church teaching on the relationship between the Church and other religions. This teaching has been deepened and developed by Pope Paul VI and most particularly by Pope John Paul II. It is not as well known as it should be. This may be because it is teaching that is both very clear and very nuanced. Central to it is the relationship and the distinction between 'dialogue' and 'proclamation'. Catholics must both proclaim the fullness of their faith and be open to the workings of the Holy Spirit in other religions. This involves developing a mind-set that is strong and balanced, so that dialogue is not pursued at the expense of mission, nor mission at the expense of dialogue.

In this booklet, Alfred Agius has put together key texts of the Church's magisterium on this matter. It is vitally important that its content be understood and appreciated as widely as possible. Although intended in the first instance for Catholic readership, the Committee for Other Faiths would hope that this material will be of service both to other Christians and to members of other religions.

+ Kevin McDonald
Bishop of Northampton
Chairman, Committee for Other Faiths

Introduction

This booklet brings together a number of documents which illustrate how the Catholic Church has progressively understood its role in a world of many faiths. The span of Church documents range from 1964, the date of the Second Vatican Council, a landmark in the life of the Catholic Church, to January 2002. It has been compiled mainly for Roman Catholics, endeavouring to convey to them the Church's attitude of respect for the rich heritage of other faiths as well as the deep spirituality of many holy people within those faiths. It is hoped that lay Catholics who engage in dialogue, clergy in their ministry, and teachers in both Catholic and state schools will find this booklet a useful resource.

Followers of other faiths as well as Christians of all traditions will find the official position of the Catholic Church explained. For them, this can serve as a sound basis to conduct research, to compare with their own tradition and to discover points of convergence. It is hoped that, in the process, we can all grow in the mutual appreciation of our different paths.

In the tradition of the Catholic Church, the form in which a particular teaching is imparted indicates its importance. In the graded order of authoritative teaching come: (1) Council documents; (2) postconciliar magisterium; (3) addresses of Popes; and (4) documents of the Roman Curia. Reference to this is given at the end of each quote. Because Roman documents on interfaith relations are often quite lengthy, only the more relevant parts of a particular document are given, indicating, at the end of each quote, the paragraph number of the original texts. Each quote has a heading which encapsulates the gist of the subject matter. (Although not strictly speaking Church teaching, some useful quotes from the International Theological Commission have been included on page 28.)

The choice of quotes is not intended to favour any particular theological position, but simply to illustrate how Pope Paul VI and, more extensively, Pope John Paul II have faithfully applied the teaching of the Council on interfaith dialogue.

The English version of most of the original texts is taken from *Interreligious Dialogue - the Official Teaching of the Catholic Church*, edited by Francesco Gioia, 1997. Later documents are taken from the Vatican Information Service. For a deeper understanding of the texts quoted the reader is well advised to go to the sources where the historical context and the wider picture enable them to get a better grasp of the Church's teaching. A list of the sources quoted is available in the index at the end of this publication, for easy reference.

I wish to thank the members of the Committee for Other Faiths for their invaluable advice in the choice of texts, and Tom Horwood of the Catholic Communications Service for his valuable advice in the presentation of this publication.

Alfred Agius

1. Basic teaching

Right to religious freedom

The Vatican Council declares that the human person has a right to religious freedom. Freedom of this kind means that all men should be immune from coercion on the part of individuals, social groups and every human power so that, within due limits, nobody is forced to act against his convictions in religious matters in private or in public, alone or in association with others. The Council further declares that the right to religious freedom is based on the very dignity of the human person as known through the revealed Word of God and by reason itself.

The right of the human person to religious freedom must be given such recognition in the constitutional order of society as will make it a civil right. ...

Everybody has the duty, and consequently the right, to seek the truth in religious matters so that, through the use of appropriate means, he may prudently form judgements of conscience which are sincere and true.

The search for truth, however, must be carried out in a manner that is appropriate to the dignity of the human person and his social nature, namely by free inquiry with the help of teaching or instruction, communication and dialogue. It is by these means that men share with each other the truth they have discovered, or think they have discovered, in such a way that they help one another in the search for truth. Moreover, it is by personal assent that men must adhere to the truth they have discovered.

It is through his conscience that man sees and recognises the demands of the divine law. He is bound to follow this conscience faithfully in all his activity so that he may come to God, who is his last end. Therefore, he must not be forced to act contrary to his conscience. Nor must he be prevented from acting according to his conscience, especially in religious matters. The reason is because the practice of religion of its very nature consists primarily of those voluntary and free internal acts by which a man directs himself to God; acts of this kind cannot be commanded or forbidden by any merely human authority. But his own social nature requires that man give external expression to these internal acts of religion, that he communicate with others on religious matters and profess his religion in community.

Consequently, to deny man the free exercise of religion in society, when the just requirements of public order are observed, is to do an injustice to the human person and to the very order established by God for men.

Furthermore, the private and public acts of religion by which men direct themselves to God according to their convictions transcend of their very nature the earthly and temporal order of things. Therefore, the civil authority, the purpose of which is the care of the common good in the temporal order, must recognise and look with favour on the religious life of the citizens. But if it presumes to control and restrict religious activity it must be said to have exceeded the limits of its power. ...

Provided that the just requirements of public order are not violated, these groups (religious communities), have a right to immunity so that they may organise themselves according to their own principles. They must be allowed to honour the supreme Godhead with public worship, help their members to practise their religion and strengthen them with religious instruction, and promote institutions in which members may work together to organise their own lives according to their religious principles.

Religious communities also have the right not to be hindered by legislation or administrative action on the part of the civil authority in the selection, training, appointment and transfer of their own ministers, in communicating with religious authorities and communities in other parts of the world, in erecting buildings for religious purposes, and in the acquisition and use of the property they need.

Religious communities have the further right not to be prevented from publicly teaching and bearing witness to their beliefs by the spoken or written word. However, in spreading religious beliefs and in introducing religious practices, everybody must at all times avoid any action which seems to suggest coercion or dishonest or unworthy persuasion, especially when dealing with the uneducated or the poor. Such a manner of acting must be considered an abuse of one's own right and an infringement of the rights of others.

Also included in the right of religious freedom is the right of religious groups not to be prevented from freely demonstrating the special value of their teaching for the organisation of society and the inspiration of all human activity. Finally, rooted in the social nature of man and in the very nature of religion is the right of men, prompted by their own religious sense, freely to hold meetings or establish educational, cultural, charitable and social organisations.

Second Vatican Council, Declaration on religious freedom, *Dignitatis Humanae*, 7 December 1965, nn. 2, 3, 4.

Relationships of respect and love

In order to bear witness to Christ, Christians should establish relationships of respect and love with those men, they should acknowledge themselves as members of the group in which they live, and through the various undertakings and affairs of human life they should share in their social and cultural life. They should be familiar with their national and religious traditions and uncover with gladness and respect those seeds of the Word which lie hidden among them. They must look at the profound transformation which is taking place among nations and work hard so that modern man is not turned away from the things of God by an excessive preoccupation with modern science and technology, but rather aroused to desire, even more intensely, that love and truth which have been revealed by God. Just as Christ penetrated to the hearts of men and by a truly human dialogue led them to the divine light, so too his disciples, profoundly pervaded by the spirit of Christ, should know and converse with those among whom they live, that through sincere and patient dialogue they themselves might learn of the riches which a generous God has distributed among the nations. They must at the same time endeavour to illuminate these riches with the light of the gospel, set them free, and bring them once more under the domination of God the saviour. …

The Church strictly forbids that anyone should be forced to accept the faith or be induced or enticed by unworthy devices; likewise, it strongly defends the right that no one should be frightened away from the faith by unjust persecutions.

Second Vatican Council, Decree on the Church's missionary activity, *Ad Gentes*, 7 December 1965, nn. 11, 13.

Eagerness for dialogue

Many people are becoming more eager to ensure that the rights of minority groups in their country be safeguarded, without overlooking the duties of these minorities toward the political community; there is also an increase in tolerance for others who differ in opinion and religion. At the same time wider cooperation is taking place to enable all citizens, and not only a few privileged individuals, to exercise their rights effectively as persons. …

With loyalty to the gospel in the fulfilment of its mission in the world, the Church, whose duty it is to foster and elevate all that is true, all that is good, and all that is beautiful in the human community (cf. *Lumen Gentium*, n. 13), consolidates peace among men for the glory of God (cf. *Luke* 2:14). ...

Our thoughts also go to all who acknowledge God and who preserve the precious religious and human elements in their traditions; it is our hope that frank dialogue will spur us all on to receive the impulses of the Spirit with fidelity and act upon them with alacrity.

For our part, our eagerness for such dialogue, conducted with appropriate discretion and leading to truth by way of love alone, excludes nobody; we would like to include those who respect outstanding human values without realising who the author of those is, as well as those who oppose the Church and persecute it in various ways. Since God the Father is the beginning and the end of all things, we are all called to be brothers; we ought to work together without violence and without deceit to build up the world in a spirit of genuine peace.

Second Vatican Council, Pastoral constitution on the Church in the modern world, *Gaudium et Spes*, 7 December 1965, nn. 73, 76, 92.

Dialogue of salvation

The dialogue of salvation was opened spontaneously on the initiative of God: 'He (God) loved us first' (*1 John* 4:1); it will be up to us to take the initiative in extending to men this same dialogue, without waiting to be summoned to it.

The dialogue of salvation began with charity, with the divine goodness: 'God so loved the world as to give his only-begotten son' (*John* 3:16). Nothing but fervent and unselfish love should motivate our dialogue.

The dialogue of salvation was not proportioned to the merits of those toward whom it was directed, nor to the results which it would achieve or fail to achieve.

The dialogue of salvation did not physically force anyone to accept it; it was a tremendous appeal of love which, although placing a vast responsibility on those toward whom it was directed (cf. *Matthew* 11:21), nevertheless left them free to respond to it or reject it. ...

The dialogue of salvation was made accessible to all; it was destined to all without distinction (cf. *Colossians* 3:11); in like manner our dialogue should be potentially universal, that is, all-embracing and capable of including all, excepting only one who would either absolutely reject it or insincerely pretend to accept it.

The dialogue of salvation normally experienced a gradual development, successive advances, humble beginnings before complete success (cf. *Matthew* 13:31). Ours, too, will take cognisance of the slowness of psychological and historical maturation and of the need to wait for the hour when God may make our dialogue effective. Not for this reason will our dialogue postpone till tomorrow what it can accomplish today; it ought to sense the preciousness of time (cf. *Ephesians* 5:16). Today, that is. Every day, our dialogue should begin again; we, rather than those towards whom it is directed, should take the initiative. ...

In the dialogue one discovers how different are the ways which lead to faith, and how it is possible to make them converge on the same goal. Even if ways are divergent, they can become complementary by forcing our reasoning process out of the worn paths and by obliging it to deepen its research, to find fresh expressions. The dialectic of this exercise of thought and of patience will make us discover elements of truth also in the opinion of others, it will force us to express our teaching with great firmness, and it will reward us for the work of having explained it in accordance with the objections of another or despite his slow assimilation of our teaching. The dialogue will make us wise; it will make us teachers.

Many, indeed, are the forms that the dialogue of salvation can take. It adapts itself to the needs of a concrete situation, it chooses the appropriate means, it does not bind itself to any ineffectual theories and does not cling to hard and fast forms when those have lost their power to speak to men and move them.

Pope Paul VI, Encyclical on the Church, *Ecclesiam Suam*, 6 August 1964, nn. 72-77, 83-84.

Positive and constructive dialogue

This new attitude has taken the name of dialogue. Dialogue is both the norm and ideal, made known to the Church by Paul VI in the encyclical *Ecclesiam Suam*. Since that time, it has been frequently used by the Council as well as in other Church teachings. It means not only discussion, but also includes all positive and constructive interreligious relations with individuals and communities of other faiths which are directed at mutual understanding and enrichment.

Through this document, the members of other religions might also come to understand better how the Church views them and how it intends to behave towards them. ...

Dialogue does not grow out of the opportunism of the tactics of the moment, but arises from reasons which experience and reflection, and even the difficulties themselves, have deepened. ...

Before all else, dialogue is a manner of acting, an attitude; a spirit which guides one's conduct. It implies concern, respect, and hospitality toward the other. It leaves room for the other person's identity, modes of expression, and values. Dialogue is thus the norm and necessary manner of every form of Christian mission, as well as of every aspect of it, whether one speaks of simple presence and witness, service, or direct proclamation (*Code of Canon Law*, can. 787.1). Any sense of mission not permeated by such a dialogical spirit would go against the demands of true humanity and against the teachings of the gospel.

Secretariat for Non-Christians (later, Pontifical Council for Interreligious Dialogue), *The Attitude of the Church Toward Followers of Other Religions*, 10 May 1984.

Dialogue and proclamation

Dialogue

Dialogue can be understood in different ways. Firstly, at the purely human level, it means reciprocal communication, leading to a common goal or, at a deeper level, to interpersonal communion. Secondly, dialogue can be taken as an attitude of respect and friendship, which should permeate all those activities constituting the evangelising mission of the Church. This can appropriately be called 'the spirit of dialogue'. Thirdly, in the context of religious plurality, dialogue means 'all positive and constructive interreligious relations with individuals and communities of other faiths which are directed to mutual understanding and enrichment' (*Attitude of the Church Toward Followers of Other Religions*), in obedience to truth and respect for freedom. It includes both the witness and exploration of respective religious convictions. It is in this third sense that the present document uses the term 'dialogue' for one of the integral elements of the Church's evangelising mission.

Forms of dialogue

There exist different forms of interreligious dialogue. It may be useful to recall those mentioned by the 1984 document of the Pontifical Council for Interreligious Dialogue. It spoke of four forms, without claiming to establish among them any order of priority:

a) The dialogue of life, where people strive to live in an open and neighbourly spirit, sharing their joys and sorrows, their human problems and preoccupations;

b) The dialogue of action, in which Christians and others collaborate for the integral development and liberation of people;

c) The dialogue of theological exchange, where specialists seek to deepen their understanding of their respective religious heritages, and to appreciate each other's spiritual values;

d) The dialogue of religious experience, where persons, rooted in their own religious traditions, share their spiritual riches, for instance with regard to prayer and contemplation, faith and ways of searching for God and the Absolute.

Obstacles to dialogue

Already on a purely human level, it is not easy to practice dialogue. Interreligious dialogue is even more difficult. It is important to be aware of the obstacles which may arise. Some would apply equally to members of all religious traditions and impede the success of dialogue. Others may affect some religious traditions more specifically and make it difficult for a process of dialogue to be initiated. Some of the more important obstacles will be mentioned here.

Human factors

a) Insufficient grounding in one's faith.

b) Insufficient knowledge and understanding of the belief and practice of those religions, leading to a lack of appreciation of their significance and even at times to misrepresentation.

c) Socio-political factors or some burdens of the past.

d) Wrong understanding of the meaning of terms such as conversion, baptism, dialogue, etc.

e) Self-sufficiency, lack of openness leading to defensive or aggressive attitudes.

f) A lack of conviction with regard to the value of interreligious dialogue, which some may see as a task reserved to specialists, and others as a sign of weakness or even a betrayal of the faith.

g) Suspicion about the other's motives in dialogue.

h) A polemical spirit when expressing religious convictions.

i) Intolerance, which is often aggravated by association with political, economic, racial and ethnic factors, a lack of reciprocity in dialogue which can lead to frustration.

j) Certain features of the present religious climate - for example: growing materialism, religious indifference, and the multiplication of religious sects, which creates confusion and raises new problems.

Why the Church engages in dialogue

Many of these obstacles arise from a lack of understanding of the true nature and goal of interreligious dialogue. These need therefore to be constantly explained. Much patience is required. It must be remembered that the Church's commitment to dialogue is not dependent on success in achieving mutual understanding and enrichment; rather it flows from God's initiative in entering into dialogue with humankind and from the example of Jesus Christ whose life, death and resurrection gave to the dialogue its ultimate expression.

Dialogue and proclamation

Interreligious dialogue and proclamation, though not on the same level, are both authentic elements of the Church's evangelising mission. Both are legitimate and necessary. They are intimately related, but not interchangeable: true interreligious dialogue on the part of the Christian supposes the desire to make Jesus Christ better known, recognised and loved; proclaiming Jesus Christ is to be carried out in the gospel spirit of dialogue. The two activities remain distinct but, as experience shows, one and the same local Church, one and the same person can be diversely engaged in both.

Pontifical Council for Interreligious Dialogue and Congregation for the Evangelisation of Peoples, *Dialogue and Proclamation*, 19 May 1991, nn. 9, 42, 51-53, 77.

Universal presence of the Holy Spirit

The Spirit, who 'blows where he wills' (cf. *John* 3:8), who 'was already at work in the world before Christ was glorified' (*Ad Gentes*, n. 4), and who 'has filled the world, ... holds all things together (and) knows what is said' (*Wisdom* 1:7), leads us to broaden our vision in order to ponder his activity in every time and place (cf. *Dominum et Vivificantem*, n. 53). I have repeatedly called this fact to mind, and it has guided me in my meetings with a wide variety of peoples. The Church's relationship with other religions is dictated by a twofold respect: 'Respect for man in his quest for answers to the deepest questions of his life, and respect for the action of the Spirit in man' (Address, Madras, 5 February 1986). Excluding any mistaken interpretation, the interreligious meeting in Assisi was meant to confirm my conviction that 'every authentic prayer is prompted by the Holy Spirit, who is mysteriously present in every human heart' (Address to cardinals, 22 December 1986).

Pope John Paul II, Encyclical on the permanent validity of the Church's missionary mandate, *Redemptoris Missio*, 7 December 1990, n. 29.

Dialogue of life

Interreligious dialogue is a part of the Church's evangelising mission. Understood as a method and means of mutual knowledge and enrichment, dialogue is not in opposition to the mission *ad gentes*; indeed it has special links with that mission and is one of its expressions. This mission, in fact, is addressed to those who do not know Christ and his gospel, and who belong for the most part to other religions. In Christ, God calls all people to himself and he wishes to share with them the fullness of his revelation and love. He does not fail to make himself present in many ways, not only to individuals but also to entire peoples through their spiritual riches, of which their religions are the main and essential expression, even when they contain 'gaps, insufficiencies and errors' (Paul VI, 29 September 1963). All of this has been given ample emphasis by the Council and the subsequent magisterium, without detracting in any way from the fact that salvation comes from Christ and that dialogue does not dispense from evangelisation. ...

A vast field lies open to dialogue, which can assume many forms and expressions: exchanges between experts in religious traditions or official representatives of those traditions; cooperation for integral development and safeguarding religious values; a sharing of respective spiritual experiences; the so-called 'dialogue of life', through which believers of different religions bear witness before each other in daily life to their own human and spiritual values and helping each other to live according to those values, in order to build a more just and fraternal society.

Each member of the faithful and all Christians communities are called to practise dialogue, although not always to the same degree, or in the same way. The contribution of the laity is indispensable in this area, for they 'can favour the relations which ought to be established with the followers of various religions through their example in the situations in which they live and in their activities' (*Christifideles Laici*, n. 35). Some of them will also be able to make a contribution through research and study.

Pope John Paul II, Encyclical on the permanent validity of the Church's missionary mandate, *Redemptoris Missio*, 7 December 1990, nn. 55, 57.

Collaborating with other religions

'And you are also witnesses' (*John* 15:27). Enlivened by the gift of the Spirit, the Church has always been keenly aware of this duty and has faithfully proclaimed the gospel message in every time and place. She has done so with respect for the dignity of peoples, of their culture, of their traditions. Indeed she knows quite well that the divine message entrusted to her is not hostile to the deepest human aspirations; indeed, it was revealed by God to satisfy, beyond every expectation, the hunger and thirst of the human heart. For this very reason the gospel must not be imposed but proposed, because it can only be effective if it is freely accepted. ...

Indeed, it is only right to listen to what the Spirit can also suggest to 'others'. They can offer useful hints for reaching a deeper understanding of what the Christian already possesses in the 'revealed deposit'. Dialogue can thus open the way to proclamation which is better suited to the personal conditions of the listener. ...

It is also clear that our firmness in being witnesses to Christ by the power of the Holy Spirit does not prevent us from collaborating in the service of man with those who belong to other religions. On the contrary, it prompts us to work together with them for the good of society and peace in the world.

Pope John Paul II, Homily on Pentecost Day, 11 June 2000.

Church rules out indifferentism

In the practice of dialogue between the Christian faith and other religious traditions as well as in seeking to understand its theoretical basis more deeply, new questions arise that need to be addressed through pursuing new paths of research, advancing proposals, and suggesting ways of acting that call for attentive discernment. In this task, the present declaration seeks to recall to bishops, theologians, and all the Catholic faithful, certain indispensable elements of Christian doctrine which may help theological reflection in developing solutions consistent with the contents of the faith and responsive to the needs of contemporary culture. The expository language of the declaration corresponds to its purpose which is not to treat in a systematic manner the question of the unicity and salvific universality of the mystery of Jesus Christ and the Church, nor to propose solutions to questions that are matters of free theological debate, but rather to set forth again the doctrine of the Catholic faith in these areas, pointing out some fundamental questions that remain open to further development, and refuting specific positions that are erroneous or ambiguous. For this reason, the declaration takes up what has been taught in previous magisterial documents, in order to reiterate certain truths that are part of the Church's faith. ...

With the coming of the Saviour Jesus Christ, God has willed that the Church founded by him be the instrument for the salvation of all humanity (cf. *Acts* 17:30-31). This truth of faith does not lessen the sincere respect which the Church has for the religions of the world, but at the same time, it rules out, in a radical way, that mentality of indifferentism 'characterised by a religious relativism which leads to the belief that "one religion is as good as another"' (*Redemptoris Missio*, n. 36). If it is true that the followers of other religions can receive divine grace, it is also certain that objectively speaking they are in a gravely deficient situation in comparison with those who, in the Church, have the fullness of the means of salvation. However, 'all the children of the Church should nevertheless remember that their exalted condition results, not from their own merits, but from the grace of Christ. If they fail to respond in thought, word, and deed to that grace, not only shall they not be saved, but they shall be more severely judged' (*Lumen Gentium*, n. 14).

Congregation for the Doctrine of the Faith, Declaration on the unicity and salvific universality of Jesus Christ and the Church, *Dominus Iesus*, 6 August 2000, nn. 3, 22.

Dialogue must continue

We should consider the great challenge of interreligious dialogue to which we shall still be committed in the new millennium, in fidelity to the teachings of the Second Vatican Council. In the years of preparation for the great jubilee the Church has sought to build, not least through a series of highly symbolic meetings, a relationship of openness and dialogue with the followers of other religions. This dialogue must continue. In the climate of increased cultural and religious pluralism which is expected to mark the society of the new millennium, it is obvious that this dialogue will be especially important in establishing a sure basis for peace and warding off the dread spectre of those wars of religion which have so often bloodied human history. The name of the one God must become increasingly what it is: a name of peace and a summons to peace.

Dialogue, however, cannot be based on religious indifferentism, and we Christians are in duty bound, while engaging in dialogue, to bear clear witness to the hope that is within us (cf. *1 Peter* 3:15). We should not fear that it will be considered an offence to the identity of others what is rather the joyful proclamation of a gift meant for all, and to be offered to all with the greatest respect for the freedom of each one: the gift of the revelation of the God who is love, the God who 'so loved the world that he gave his only Son' (*John* 3:16). As the recent declaration *Dominus Iesus* stressed, this cannot be the subject of a dialogue understood as negotiation, as if we considered it a matter of mere opinion: rather, it is a grace which fills us with joy, a message which we have a duty to proclaim.

The Church therefore cannot forgo her missionary activity among the peoples of the world. It is the primary task of the *missio ad gentes* to announce that it is in Christ, 'the way, and the truth, and the life' (*John* 14:6), that people find salvation. Interreligious dialogue 'cannot simply replace proclamation, but remains oriented towards proclamation' (*Dialogue and Proclamation*, n. 82). This missionary duty, moreover, does not prevent us from approaching dialogue with an attitude of profound willingness to listen. We know in fact that, in the presence of the mystery of grace, infinitely full of possibilities and implications for human life and history, the Church herself will never cease putting questions, trusting in the help of the Paraclete, the Spirit of truth (cf. *John* 14:17), whose task it is to guide her 'into all the truth' (*John* 16:13).

This is a fundamental principle not only for the endless theological investigation of Christian truth, but also for Christian dialogue with other philosophies, cultures and religions. In the common experience of humanity, for all its contradictions, the Spirit of God, who 'blows where he wills' (*John* 3:8), not infrequently reveals signs of his presence which help Christ's followers to understand more deeply the message which they bear. Was it not with this humble and trust-filled openness that the Second Vatican Council sought to read 'the signs of the times' (*Gaudium et Spes*, n. 4)? Even as she engages in an active and watchful discernment aimed at understanding the 'genuine signs of the presence or the purpose of God' (*Gaudium et Spes*, n. 11), the Church acknowledges that she has not only given, but has also 'received from the history and from the development of the human race' (*Gaudium et Spes*, n. 44). This attitude of openness, combined with careful discernment, was adopted by the Council also in relation to other religions. It is our task to follow with great fidelity the Council's teaching and the path which it has traced.

Pope John Paul II, Apostolic letter at the close of the great jubilee year 2000, *Novo Millennio Ineunte*, 6 January 2001, nn. 55-56.

2. All faiths

Church rejects nothing true and holy

In this age of ours, when men are drawing more closely together and the bonds of friendship between different peoples are being strengthened, the Church examines with greater care the relation which she has to non-Christian religions. Ever aware of her duty to foster unity and charity among individuals, and even among nations, she reflects at the outset on what men have in common and what tends to promote fellowship among them. ...

All men form but one community. This is so because all stem from the one stock which God created to people the entire earth (cf. *Acts* 17:26) and also because all share a common destiny, namely God. ...

The Catholic Church rejects nothing of what is true and holy in these religions. She has a high regard for the manner of life and conduct, the precepts and doctrines, which, although differing in many ways from her own teaching, nevertheless often reflect a ray of that truth which enlightens all men. Yet she proclaims and is in duty bound to proclaim without fail, Christ who is 'the way, the truth and the life' (*John* 1:6). In him, in whom God reconciled all things to himself (cf. *2 Corinthians* 5:18-19), men find the fullness of their religious life. The Church, therefore, urges her sons to enter with prudence and charity into discussion and collaboration with members of other religions. Let Christians, while witnessing to their own faith and way of life, acknowledge, preserve and encourage the spiritual and moral truths found among non-Christians, also their social life and culture. ...

We cannot truly pray to God the Father of all if we treat any people in other than brotherly fashion, for all men are created in God's image. Man's relation to God the Father and man's relation to his fellow men are so dependent on each other that the scripture says, 'he who does not love, does not know God' (*1 John* 4:8). There is no basis, therefore, either in theory or in practice, for any discrimination between individual and individual, or between people, arising either from human dignity or from the rights which flow from it. Therefore, the Church reproves, as foreign to the mind of Christ, any discrimination against people, or any harassment of them on the basis of their race, colour, conditions in life or religion.

Second Vatican Council, Declaration on the relationship of the Church to non-Christian religions, *Nostra Aetate*, 28 October 1965, nn. 1, 2, 5.

Those who have not received the gospel

Finally, those who have not yet received the gospel are related to the People of God in various ways. There is, first, that people to which the covenants and promises were made, and from which Christ was born according to the flesh (cf. *Romans* 9:4-5): in view of the divine choice, they are a people most dear for the sake of the fathers, for the gifts of God are without repentance (cf. *Romans* 11:28-29). But the plan of salvation also includes those who acknowledge the Creator, in the first place among whom are the Muslims: these profess to hold the faith of Abraham, and together with us they adore the one, merciful God, mankind's judge on the last day. Nor is God remote from those who in shadows and images seek the unknown God, since he gives to all life and breath and all things (cf. *Acts* 17:25-28), and since the Saviour wills all men to be saved (cf. *1 Timothy* 2-4). Those who, through no fault of their own, do not know the gospel of Christ or his Church, but who nevertheless seek God with a sincere heart, and moved by grace, try in their actions to do his will as they know it through the dictates of their conscience - those too, may achieve eternal salvation. Nor shall divine providence deny the assistance necessary for salvation to those who without any fault of theirs have not yet arrived at an explicit knowledge of God, and who, not without grace, strive to lead a good life. Whatever good or truth is found among them is considered by the Church to be a preparation for the gospel and given by him who enlightens all men that they may at length have life. But very often, deceived by the Evil One, men have become vain in their reasoning, have exchanged the truth of God for a lie and have served the world rather than the Creator (cf. *Roman* 1:21,25), or else, living and dying in this world without God, they are exposed to ultimate despair. Hence, to procure the glory of God and the salvation of all these, the Church, mindful of the Lord's command, 'preach the gospel to every creature' (*Mark* 16:15), takes zealous care to foster missions.

Second Vatican Council, Dogmatic constitution on the Church, *Lumen Gentium*, 21 November 1964, n. 16.

Secretariat for Non-Christians

The Secretariat for Non-Christians ... is to effectively reach those who are not Christians but who profess some religion or a religious sense. ... It is up to this secretariat to seek ways and means of establishing a suitable dialogue with non-Christians. It should receive and examine the wishes of ordinaries; provide for the training of those who will engage in dialogue; propose initiatives, examine them and approve those proved useful by experience.

Pope Paul VI, Apostolic constitution establishing the Secretariat for Non-Christians (later, Pontifical Council for Interreligious Dialogue), *Regimini Ecclesiae Universae*, 15 August 1967, nn. 96, 99.

Esteem for great spiritual values

The Council document on non-Christian religions, in particular, is filled with deep esteem for the great spiritual values, indeed for the primacy of the spiritual, which in the life of mankind finds expression in religion and then in morality, with direct effects on the whole of culture. The fathers of the Church rightly saw in the various religions so many reflections of the one truth, 'seeds of the Word' attesting that, though the routes taken may be different, there is but a single goal to which is directed the deepest aspiration of the human spirit, as expressed in its quest for God and also in its quest, through its tending toward God, for the full dimension of its humanity, or in other words for the full meaning of human life. The Council gave particular attention to the Jewish religion, recalling the great spiritual heritage common to Christians and Jews. It also expressed its esteem for the believers of Islam, whose faith also looks to Abraham (cf. *Nostra Aetate*, nn. 3-4).

Pope John Paul II, Encyclical on redemption and dignity of the human race, *Redemptor Hominis*, 4 March 1979, n. 11.

Interfaith marriages

Today in many parts of the world marriages between Catholics and non-baptised persons are growing in numbers. In many such marriages the non-baptised partner professes another religion, and his beliefs are to be treated with respect, in accordance with the principles set out in the Second Vatican Council's declaration *Nostra Aetate* on relations with non-Christian religions.

Pope John Paul II, Apostolic exhortation on the role of the Christian family in the modern world, *Familiaris Consortio*, 22 November 1981, n. 81.

Walk together in peace and harmony

The very fact that we have come to Assisi from various parts of the world is in itself a sign of this common path which humanity is called to tread. Either we learn to walk together in peace and harmony, or we drift apart and ruin ourselves and others. We hope that this pilgrimage to Assisi has taught us anew to be aware of the common origin and common destiny of humanity. Let us see in it an anticipation of what God would like the developing history of humanity to be: a fraternal journey in which we accompany one another toward the transcendent goal which he sets for us.

Pope John Paul II, Address at World Day for Peace, Assisi, 27 October 1986, n. 5.

Lay Catholics and other religions

The Synod fathers have mentioned that the lay faithful can favour the relations which ought to be established with followers of various religions through their example in the situations in which they live and in their activities (proposition 30): 'Throughout the world today the Church lives among people of various religions. ... All the faithful, especially the lay faithful who live among people of other religions, whether living in their native region or in lands as migrants, ought to be for all a sign of the Lord and his Church, in a way adapted to the actual living situation of each place. Dialogue among religions has a pre-eminent part, for it leads to love and mutual respect, and takes away, or at least diminishes, prejudices among the followers of various religions, and promotes unity and friendship among peoples.'

Pope John Paul II, Apostolic exhortation on the vocation and mission of the lay faithful, *Christifideles Laici*, 20 December 1988, n. 35.

Dialogue in year 2000

As far as the field of religious awareness is concerned, the eve of the year 2000 will provide a great opportunity, especially in view of the events of recent decades, for interreligious dialogue, in accordance with the specific guidelines set down by the Second Vatican Council in its declaration *Nostra Aetate* on the relationship of the Church to non-Christian religions.

In this dialogue the Jews and the Muslims ought to have a pre-eminent place. God grant that, as a confirmation of these intentions, it may also be possible to hold joint meetings in places of significance for the great monotheistic religions. ...

However, care will also have to be taken not to cause harmful misunderstandings, avoiding the risk of syncretism and of a facile and deceptive irenicism.

Pope John Paul II, Apostolic letter on preparation for the jubilee year 2000, *Tertio Millennio Adveniente*, 10 November 1994, n. 52.

Promote a culture of dialogue

I have always believed that religious leaders have a vital role to play in nurturing that hope of justice and peace without which there will be no future worthy of humanity. As the world marks the close of one millennium and the opening of another, it is right that we take time to look back, in order to take stock of the present situation and move forward together in hope towards the future.

As we survey the situation of humanity, is it too much to speak of a crisis of civilisation? We see great technological advances, but these are not always accompanied by great spiritual and moral progress. We see as well a growing gap between the rich and poor - at the level of individuals and of nations. Many people make great sacrifices to show solidarity with those suffering want or hunger or disease, but there is still lacking the collective will to overcome scandalous inequalities and to create new structures which will enable all peoples to have a just share in the world's resources.

Then there are the many conflicts continually breaking out around the world: wars between nations, armed struggles within nations, conflicts that linger like festering wounds and cry out for a healing that seems never to come. Inevitably it is the weakest who suffer most in these conflicts, especially when they are uprooted from their homes and forced to flee.

Surely this is not the way humanity is supposed to live. Is it not therefore right to say that there is indeed a crisis of civilisation which can be countered only by a new civilisation of love, founded on the universal values of peace, solidarity, justice and liberty?

There are some who claim that religion is part of the problem, blocking humanity's way to true peace and prosperity. As religious people, it is our duty to demonstrate that this is not the case. Any use of religion to support violence is an abuse of religion. Religion is not and must not become a pretext for conflict, particularly when religious, cultural and ethnic identity coincide. Religion and peace go together: to wage war in the name of religion is a blatant contradiction. Religious leaders must clearly show that they are pledged to promote peace precisely because of their religious belief.

The task before us therefore is to promote a culture of dialogue. Individually and together, we must show how religious belief inspires peace, encourages solidarity, promotes justice and upholds liberty.

But teaching itself is never enough, however indispensable it may be. It must be translated into action. My revered predecessor Pope Paul VI noted that in our time people pay more attention to witnesses than to teachers, that they listen to teachers if they are at the same time witnesses (cf. *Evangelii Nuntiandi*, n. 41). It suffices to think of the unforgettable witness of people like Mahatma Gandhi or Mother Teresa of Calcutta, to mention but two figures who have had such an impact on the world.

Moreover, the strength of witness lies in the fact that it is shared. It is a sign of hope that in many parts of the world interreligious associations have been established to promote joint reflection and action. In some places, religious leaders have been instrumental in mediating between warring parties. Elsewhere, common cause is made to protect the unborn, to uphold the rights of women and children, and to defend the innocent. I am convinced that the increased interest in dialogue between religions is one of the signs of hope present in the last part of this century. Yet there is a need to go further. Greater mutual esteem and growing trust must lead to still more effective and coordinated common action on behalf of the human family.

Our hope rises not merely from the capacities of the human heart and mind, but has a divine dimension which it is right to recognise. Those of us who are Christians believe that this hope is a gift of the Holy Spirit, who calls us to widen our horizons, to look beyond our own personal needs and the needs of our particular communities, to the unity of the whole human family. The teaching and example of Jesus Christ have given Christians a clear sense of the universal brotherhood of all people. Awareness that the Spirit of God works where he wills (cf. *John* 3:8) stops us from making hasty and dangerous judgements, because it evokes appreciation of what lies hidden in the hearts of others. This opens the way to reconciliation, harmony and peace. From this spiritual awareness springs compassion and generosity, humility and modesty, courage and perseverance. These are qualities that humanity needs more than ever as it moves into the new millennium.

Pope John Paul II, Address at the Interreligious Assembly, Rome, 28 October 1999, nn. 2-4.

Religion and peace

Each of our religions knows, in some form or another, the Golden Rule: Do unto others as you would have them do unto you. Precious as this rule is as a guide, true love of neighbour goes much further. It is based on the conviction that when we love our neighbour we are showing love for God, and when we hurt our neighbour we offend God. This means that religion is the enemy of exclusion and discrimination, of hatred and rivalry, of violence and conflict. Religion is not, and must not become, an excuse for violence, particularly when religious identity coincides with cultural and ethnic identity. Religion and peace go together! Religious belief and practice cannot be separated from the defence of the image of God in every human being.

Drawing upon the riches of our respective religious traditions, we must spread awareness that today's problems will not be solved if we remain ignorant of one another and isolated from one another. We are all aware of past misunderstandings and conflicts, and these still weigh heavily upon relationships between Jews, Christians and Muslims. We must do all we can to turn awareness of past offences and sins into a firm resolve to build a new future in which there will be nothing but respectful and fruitful cooperation between us.

The Catholic Church wishes to pursue a sincere and fruitful interreligious dialogue with the members of the Jewish faith and the followers of Islam. Such a dialogue is not an attempt to impose our views upon others. What it demands of all of us is that, holding to what we believe, we listen respectfully to one another, seek to discern all that is good and holy in each other's teachings, and cooperate in supporting everything that favours mutual understanding and peace.

Pope John Paul II, To Christian, Jewish and Muslim leaders, Jerusalem, 23 March 2000.

Request for pardon

On the interreligious level, it is appropriate to point out that, for believers in Christ, the Church's recognition of past wrongs is consistent with the requirements of fidelity to the gospel, and therefore constitutes a shining witness of faith in the truth and mercy of God as revealed by Jesus. What must be avoided is that these acts be mistaken as confirmation of possible prejudices against Christianity. It would also be desirable if these acts of repentance would stimulate the members of other religions to acknowledge the faults of their own past. Just as the history of humanity is full of violence, genocide, violations of human rights and the rights of peoples, exploitation of the weak and glorification of the powerful, so too the history of the various religions is marked by intolerance, superstition, complicity with unjust powers, and the denial of the dignity and freedom of conscience. Christians have been no exception and they are aware that all are sinners before God!

International Theological Commission, *Memory and Reconciliation: the Church and the faults of the past*, 7 March 2000, n. 6.3.

Let us forgive and ask forgiveness! While we praise God who, in his merciful love, has produced in the Church a wonderful harvest of holiness, missionary zeal, total dedication to Christ and neighbour, we cannot fail to recognise the infidelities to the gospel committed by some of our brethren, especially during the second millennium. Let us ask pardon for the divisions which have occurred among Christians, for the violence some have used in the service of the truth and for the distrustful and hostile attitudes sometimes taken towards the followers of other religions.

Pope John Paul II, Homily for Day of Pardon, 12 March 2000, n. 4.

Forgiveness, justice and freedom

In this whole effort [for peace], religious leaders have a weighty responsibility. The various Christian confessions, as well as the world's great religions, need to work together to eliminate the social and cultural causes of terrorism. They can do this by teaching the greatness and dignity of the human person, and by spreading a clearer sense of the oneness of the human family. This is a specific area of ecumenical and interreligious dialogue and cooperation, a pressing service which religion can offer to world peace. In particular, I am convinced that Jewish, Christian and Islamic religious leaders must now take the lead in publicly condemning terrorism and in denying terrorists any form of religious or moral legitimacy.

In bearing common witness to the truth that the deliberate murder of the innocent is a grave evil always, everywhere, and without exception, the world's religious leaders will help to form the morally sound public opinion that is essential for building an international civil society capable of pursuing the tranquility of order in justice and freedom. In undertaking such a commitment, the various religions cannot but pursue the path of forgiveness, which opens the way to mutual understanding, respect and trust. The help that religions can give to peace and against terrorism consists precisely in their teaching forgiveness, for those who forgive and seek forgiveness know that there is a higher truth, and that by accepting that truth they can transcend themselves.

Pope John Paul II, Message for World Day for Peace 2002, 8 December 2001, nn. 12-13.

Interreligious meeting 2002

It is my intention to invite the representatives of the religions of the world to come to Assisi on 24 January 2002 to pray that opposing positions be overcome and that an authentic peace be promoted. We hope to see in practice, Christians and Muslims, to proclaim before the world that religion must never become a motive of conflict, hatred and violence. ... Whoever welcomes the word of God, who is good and merciful, must exclude from their heart every form of bitter hatred and enmity. In this historical moment, mankind needs to see gestures of peace and to listen to prayers of hope.

Pope John Paul II, To pilgrims in St Peter's Square, Rome, 18 November 2001.

We have come to Assisi on a pilgrimage of peace. We are here, as representatives of different religions, to examine ourselves before God concerning our commitment to peace, to ask him for this gift, to bear witness to our shared longing for a world of greater justice and solidarity. We wish to do our part in fending off the dark clouds of terrorism, hatred, armed conflict, which in these last few months have grown particularly ominous on humanity's horizon. For this reason we wish to listen to one other: we believe that this itself is already a sign of peace. In listening to one another there is already a reply to the disturbing questions that worry us. This already serves to scatter the shadows of suspicion and misunderstanding. The shadows will not be dissipated with weapons; darkness is dispelled by sending out bright beams of light. A few days ago I reminded the diplomatic corps accredited to the Holy See that hatred can only be overcome through love.

Pope John Paul II, To representatives of world religions, Assisi, 24 January 2002.

3. Judaism

Common spiritual patrimony

As the sacred synod searches into the mystery of the Church, it remembers the bond that spiritually ties the people of the New Covenant to Abraham's stock. Thus the Church of Christ acknowledges that, according to God's saving design, the beginnings of her faith and her election are found already among the patriarchs, Moses and the prophets. She professes that all who believe in Christ - Abraham's sons according to faith (cf. *Galatians* 3:7) - are included in the same Patriarch's call, and likewise that the salvation of the Church is mysteriously foreshadowed by the chosen people's exodus from the land of bondage. The Church, therefore, cannot forget that she received the revelation of the Old Testament through the people with whom God in his inexpressible mercy concluded the Ancient Covenant. Nor can she forget that she draws sustenance from the root of that well-cultivated olive tree onto which have been grafted the wild shoots, the Gentiles (cf. *Romans* 11:17-24). Indeed, the Church believes that by his cross Christ, our peace, reconciled Jews and Gentiles, making both one in himself (cf. *Ephesians* 2:14-16).

The Church keeps ever in mind the words of the Apostle about his kinsmen: 'theirs is the sonship and the glory and the covenants and the law and the worship and the promises; theirs are the fathers and from them is the Christ according to the flesh' (*Romans* 9:4-5), the Son of the Virgin Mary. She also recalls that the Apostles, the Church's mainstay and pillars, as well as most of the early disciples who proclaimed Christ's gospel to the world, sprang from the Jewish people.

As Holy Scripture testifies, Jerusalem did not recognise the time of her visitation (cf. *Luke* 19:44), nor did the Jews in large number, accept the gospel; indeed not a few opposed its spreading (cf. *Romans* 11:28). Nevertheless, God holds the Jews most dear for the sake of their Fathers; he does not repent of the gifts he makes or of the calls he issues - such is the witness of the Apostle (cf. *Romans* 11:28-29). In company with the prophets and the same Apostle, the Church awaits that day, known to God alone, on which all peoples will address the Lord in a single voice and 'serve him shoulder to shoulder' (*Zephaniah* 3:9).

Since the spiritual patrimony common to Christians and Jews is thus so great, this sacred synod wants to foster and recommend that mutual understanding and respect which is the fruit, above all, of biblical and theological studies as well as of fraternal dialogues.

True, the Jewish authorities and those who followed their lead pressed for the death of Christ (cf. *John* 19:6); still, what happened in his passion cannot be charged against all the Jews, without distinction, then alive, nor against the Jews of today. Although the Church is the new people of God, the Jews should not be presented as rejected or accursed by God, as if this followed from the holy scriptures. All should see to it, then, that in catechetical work or in the preaching of the word of God they do not teach anything that does not conform to the truth of the gospel and the spirit of Christ.

Furthermore, in her rejection of every persecution against any man, the Church, mindful of the patrimony she shares with the Jews and moved not by political reasons but by the gospel's spiritual love, decries hatred, persecutions, displays of anti-Semitism, directed against Jews at any time and by anyone.

Besides, as the Church has always held and holds now, Christ underwent his passion and death freely, because of the sins of men and out of infinite love, in order that all may reach salvation. It is, therefore, the burden of the Church's preaching to proclaim the cross of Christ as the sign of God's all-embracing love and as the fountain from which every grace flows.

Second Vatican Council, Declaration on the relationship of the Church to non-Christian religions, *Nostra Aetate*, 28 October 1965, n. 4.

Relations between two communities

The links between the Church and the Jewish people are founded on the design of the God of the Covenant and - as such - have necessarily left their traces in certain aspects of the institutions of the Church, particularly in her liturgy. Certainly, since the appearance, two thousand years ago, of a new branch from the common root, relations between our two communities have been marked by the misunderstandings and resentments with which we are familiar. And if, since the day of the separation, there have been misunderstandings, errors, indeed offences, it is now our task to leave these behind with understanding, peace, and mutual respect. The terrible persecution suffered by the Jews in different periods of history have finally opened the eyes of many and appalled many people's hearts. Christians have taken the right path, that of justice and brotherhood, in seeking to come together with their Semitic brethren, respectfully and perseveringly, in the common heritage that all value so highly. Should it not be pointed out, especially to those who remain sceptical, even hostile, that this reconciliation should not be confused with a sort of religious relativism, less still with a loss of identity? Christians, for their part, profess their faith unequivocally in the universal salvific significance of the death and resurrection of Jesus of Nazareth.

Pope John Paul II, To representatives of episcopal conferences and other experts in Catholic-Jewish relations, 6 March 1982.

Abhorrence for genocide

This gathering in a way brings to a close, after the pontificate of John XXIII and the Second Vatican Council, a long period which we must not tire of reflecting upon in order to draw appropriate lessons from it. Certainly we cannot and should not forget that the historical circumstances of the past were very different from those that have laboriously matured over the centuries. The general acceptance of a legitimate plurality on the social, civil and religious levels has been arrived at with great difficulty. Nevertheless, a consideration of centuries-long cultural conditioning could not prevent us from recognising that acts of discrimination, unjustified limitations of religious freedom, oppression also on the level of civil freedom in regards to the Jews were, from an objective point of view, gravely deplorable manifestations. Yes, once again, through myself, the Church, in the words of the well known declaration *Nostra Aetate*, 'deplores the hatred, persecutions, and displays of anti-Semitism directed against the Jews at any time and by anyone'; I repeat: 'by anyone' (n. 4).

I would like once more to express a word of abhorrence for the genocide decreed against the Jewish people during the last war, which led to the holocaust of millions of innocent victims. ...

It must be said, then, that the ways opened for our collaboration, in the light of our common heritage, drawn from the Law and the prophets, are various and important. We wish to recall first of all, a collaboration in favour of man, his life from conception until natural death, his dignity, freedom, rights and self-development in a society which is not hostile but friendly and favourable, where justice reigns and where, in this nation, on the various continents and throughout the world, peace rules, the *shalom* hoped for by the lawmakers, prophets and wise men of Israel.

More in general, there is the problem of morality, the great field of individual and social ethics. We are all aware of how acute the crisis is on this point in the age in which we are living. In a society which is often lost in agnosticism and individualism and which is suffering the bitter consequences of selfishness and violence, Jews and Christians are the trustees of an ethic marked by the Ten Commandments, in the observance of which man finds his truth and freedom. To promote a common reflection and collaboration on this point is one of the great duties of the hour. ...

I venture to say, we shall each be faithful to our most sacred commitments, and also to that which most profoundly unites and gathers us together: faith in the one God who 'loves strangers' and 'renders justice to the orphan and the widow' (cf. *Deuteronomy* 10:18), commanding us also to love and help them. Christians have learned this desire of the Lord from the *Torah*, which you here venerate, and from Jesus who took to its extreme consequences the love demanded by the *Torah*.

Pope John Paul II, To representatives of the Jewish community of Rome, 13 April 1986.

Anti-Semitism and the Holocaust

We cannot ignore the difference which exists between anti-Semitism, based on theories contrary to the constant teaching of the Church on the unity of the human race and on the equal dignity of all races and peoples, and the long-standing sentiments of mistrust and hostility that we call anti-Judaism, of which, unfortunately, Christians also have been guilty.

The National Socialist ideology went even further, in the sense that it refused to acknowledge any transcendent reality as the source of life and the criterion of moral good. Consequently, a human group, and the State with which it was identified, abrogated to itself an absolute status and determined to remove the very existence of the Jewish people, a people called to witness to the one God and the Law of the Covenant. At the level of theological reflection we cannot ignore the fact that not a few in the Nazi Party not only showed aversion to the idea of divine Providence at work in human affairs, but gave proof of a definite hatred directed at God himself. Logically, such an attitude also led to a rejection of Christianity, and a desire to see the Church destroyed or at least subjected to the interests of the Nazi State.

It was this extreme ideology which became the basis of the measures taken, first to drive the Jews from their homes and then to exterminate them. The *Shoah* [Holocaust] was the work of a thoroughly modern neo-pagan regime. Its anti-Semitism had its roots outside of Christianity and, in pursuing its aims, it did not hesitate to oppose the Church and persecute her members also.

But it may be asked whether the Nazi persecution of the Jews was not made easier by the anti-Jewish prejudices imbedded in some Christian minds and hearts. Did anti-Jewish sentiment among Christians make them less sensitive, or even indifferent, to the persecutions launched against the Jews by National Socialism when it reached power?

Any response to this question must take into account that we are dealing with the history of people's attitudes and ways of thinking, subject to multiple influences. Moreover, many people were altogether unaware of the 'final solution' that was being put into effect against a whole people; others were afraid for themselves and those near to them; some took advantage of the situation; and still others were moved by envy. A response would need to be given case by case. To do this, however, it is necessary to know what precisely motivated people in a particular situation. ...

Did Christians give every possible assistance to those being persecuted, and in particular to the persecuted Jews? Many did, but others did not. Those who did help to save Jewish lives as much as was in their power, even to the point of placing their own lives in danger, must not be forgotten. During and after the war, Jewish communities and Jewish leaders expressed their thanks for all that had been done for them, including what Pope Pius XII did personally or through his representatives to save hundreds of thousands of Jewish lives. Many Catholic bishops, priests, religious and laity have been honoured for this reason by the State of Israel.

Nevertheless, as Pope John Paul II has recognised, alongside such courageous men and women, the spiritual resistance and concrete action of other Christians was not that which might have been expected from Christ's followers. We cannot know how many Christians in countries occupied or ruled by the Nazi powers or their allies were horrified at the disappearance of their Jewish neighbours and yet were not strong enough to raise their voices in protest. For Christians, this heavy burden of conscience of their brothers and sisters during the Second World War must be a call to penitence.

We deeply regret the errors and failures of those sons and daughters of the Church. We make our own what is said in the Second Vatican Council's declaration *Nostra Aetate*, which unequivocally affirms: 'The Church … mindful of her common patrimony with the Jews, and motivated by the gospel's spiritual love and by no political considerations, deplores the hatred, persecutions and displays of anti-Semitism directed against the Jews at any time and from any source'. We recall and abide by what Pope John Paul II, addressing the leaders of the Jewish community in Strasbourg in 1988, stated: 'I repeat again with you the strongest condemnation of anti-Semitism and racism, which are opposed to the principles of Christianity' (address to Jewish leaders, Strasbourg, 9 October 1988). The Catholic Church therefore repudiates every persecution against a people or human group anywhere, at any time. She absolutely condemns all forms of genocide, as well as the racist ideologies which give rise to them. …

Looking to the future of relations between Jews and Christians, in the first place we appeal to our Catholic brothers and sisters to renew the awareness of the Hebrew roots of their faith. We ask them to keep in mind that Jesus was a descendant of David; that the Virgin Mary and the Apostles belonged to the Jewish people; that the Church draws sustenance from the root of that good olive tree on to which have been grafted the wild olive branches of the Gentiles (cf. *Romans* 11:17-24); that the Jews are our dearly beloved brothers, indeed in a certain sense they are 'our elder brothers' (Pope John Paul II, speech at synagogue of Rome, 13 April 1986).

At the end of this millennium the Catholic Church desires to express her deep sorrow for the failures of her sons and daughters in every age. This is an act of repentance (*teshuva*), since, as members of the Church, we are linked to the sins as well as the merits of all her children. The Church approaches with deep respect and great compassion the experience of extermination, the *Shoah*, suffered by the Jewish people during World War II. It is not a matter of mere words, but indeed of binding commitment. 'We would risk causing the victims of the most atrocious deaths to die again if we do not have an ardent desire for justice, if we do not commit ourselves to ensure that evil does not prevail over good as it did for millions of the children of the Jewish people. … Humanity cannot permit all that to happen again' (Pope John Paul II, address on commemoration of the *Shoah*, 7 April 1994).

We pray that our sorrow for the tragedy which the Jewish people has suffered in our century will lead to a new relationship with the Jewish people. We wish to turn awareness of past sins into a firm resolve to build a new future in which there will be no more anti-Judaism among Christians or anti-Christian sentiment among Jews, but rather a shared mutual respect, as befits those who adore the one Creator and Lord and have a common father in faith, Abraham.

Finally, we invite all men and women of good will to reflect deeply on the significance of the *Shoah*. The victims from their graves, and the survivors through the vivid testimony of what they have suffered, have become a loud voice calling the attention of all of humanity. To remember this terrible experience is to become fully conscious of the salutary warning it entails: the spoiled seeds of anti-Judaism and anti-Semitism must never again be allowed to take root in any human heart.

Commission for Religious Relations with the Jews, *We Remember: a reflection on the Shoah*, 16 March 1998, nn. 4, 5.

Collaboration in proclaiming God's plan

This dialogical attitude between Christians and Jews not only expresses the general value of interreligious dialogue, but also the long journey they share leading from the Old to the New Testament. There is a long period of salvation history which Christians and Jews can view together. 'The Jewish faith', in fact, 'unlike other non-Christians religions, is already a response to God's revelation in the Old Covenant' (*Catechism of the Catholic Church*, n. 839). ...

Today the courageous witness of faith should also mark the collaboration of Christians and Jews in proclaiming and realising God's saving plan for all humanity. If his plan is interpreted in a different way regarding the acceptance of Christ, this obviously involves a crucial difference which is at the very origin of Christianity itself, but does not change the fact that there are still many elements in common.

It still is our duty to work together in promoting a human condition that more closely conforms to God's plan. The great jubilee of the year 2000, which refers precisely to the Jewish tradition of jubilee years, points to the urgent need of this common effort to restore peace and social justice. Recognising God's dominion over all creation, particularly the earth (*Leviticus* 25), all believers are called to translate their faith into a practical commitment to protecting the sacredness of human life in all its forms and to defending the dignity of every brother and sister.

In meditating on the mystery of Israel and its 'irrevocable calling', Christians also explore the mystery of their own roots. In the biblical sources they share with their Jewish brothers and sisters, they find the indispensable elements for living and deepening their own faith. ...

Not only the shared history of Christians and Jews, but especially their dialogue must look to the future (cf. *Catechism*, n. 840), becoming as it were a '*memoria futuri*' (*We Remember: A Reflection on the Shoah*, 16 March 1998, n. 1). The memory of these sorrowful and tragic events of the past can open the way to a renewed sense of brotherhood, the fruit of God's grace, and to working so that the seeds infected with anti-Judaism and anti-Semitism will never again take root in human hearts.

Pope John Paul II, General audience, 28 April 1999.

Pray for peace and justice

I have come to Yad Vashem to pay homage to the millions of Jewish people who, stripped of everything, especially of their human dignity, were murdered in the Holocaust. More than half a century has passed, but the memories remain. ...

Jews and Christians share an immense spiritual patrimony, flowing from God's self revelation. Our religious teaching and our spiritual experience demand that we overcome evil with good. We remember, but not with any desire for vengeance or as an incentive to hatred. For us to remember is to pray for peace and justice, and to commit ourselves to their cause. Only a world at peace, with justice for all, can avoid repeating the mistakes and terrible crimes of the past.

As Bishop of Rome and successor of the Apostle Peter, I assure the Jewish people that the Catholic Church, motivated by the gospel law of truth and love and by no political considerations, is deeply saddened by the hatred, acts of persecution and displays of anti-Semitism directed against the Jews by Christians at any time and in any place. The Church rejects racism in any form as a denial of the image of the Creator inherent in every human being (cf. *Genesis* 1:26).

Pope John Paul II, At the Yad Vashem Mausoleum, Jerusalem, 23 March 2000.

4. Islam

High regard for Muslims

The Church has also a high regard for the Muslims. They worship God, who is one, living and subsistent, merciful and almighty, the Creator of heaven and earth who has also spoken to men. They strive to submit themselves without reserve to the hidden decrees of God, just as Abraham submitted himself to God's plan, to whose faith Muslims eagerly link their own. Although not acknowledging him as God, they venerate Jesus as a prophet, his Virgin Mother they also honour, and even at times devoutly invoke. Further, they await the day of judgement and the reward of God following the resurrection of the dead. For this reason they highly esteem an upright life and worship God, especially by way of prayer, alms-deeds and fasting.

Over the centuries many quarrels and dissensions have arisen between Christians and Muslims. The sacred Council now pleads with all to forget the past, and urge that a sincere effort be made to achieve mutual understanding; for the benefit of all men, let them together preserve and promote peace, liberty, social justice and moral values.

Second Vatican Council, Declaration on the relationship of the Church to non-Christian religions, *Nostra Aetate*, 28 October 1965, n. 3.

Need for dialogue

One of the essential characteristics of the life of the Church in Maghreb is, in fact, to be invited to enter upon a constructive Islamic-Christian dialogue. I am anxious to encourage you along this difficult way, where failure may occur, but where hope is even stronger. To maintain it, strong Christian convictions are necessary. More than elsewhere, it is highly desirable that Christians should take part, as you encourage them to do, in a permanent catechesis which completes a biblical renewal course, or more exactly a reading of the Word of God in the Church, with the help of theologians and truly competent spiritual teachers.

But it can never be said enough that such a dialogue is in the first place a question of friendship; one must know how to give dialogue the time for progress and discernment. That is why it is surrounded by discretion out of a concern to be considerate with regard to the slowness of the evolution of mentalities.

The seriousness of commitment in this dialogue is measured by that of the witness lived and borne to the values in which one believes, and, for the Christian, to him who is their foundation, Jesus Christ. That is why it conceals an inevitable tension between the deep respect which is due to the person and the convictions of the one with whom we are speaking, and an unshakeable attachment to one's faith. This sincere dialogue and this demanding witness involve a part of spiritual abnegation: how can we fail to proclaim the hope that we have received of taking part in this wedding feast of the Lamb at which the whole of mankind will be gathered one day?

It is also necessary - among other things, in order to preserve this dialogue in its truth - for this deep hope to remain without yielding to any faintheartedness born of uncertain doctrine. Such a spirit is embodied in the first place in disinterested service with a view to fraternity participating in the development of these countries and to sharing the aspirations of their people. I am anxious to stress here the quality of the work carried out by so many of these cooperators in discretion and dedication, and by those who supported them.

Pope John Paul II, To the bishops of North Africa on their *ad limina* visit, Rome, 23 November 1981.

Promote dialogue

In this country, which is mainly Muslim, you take care to keep alive in Christians the sense of friendship, a friendship whose sincerity is measured by the effectiveness of the actions it inspires. I do not want to dwell here on this important question of the dialogue between Christians and Muslims, with which I quite recently dealt in my conversations with your confreres in North Africa. But I am anxious to point out the importance of the initiative you have taken in common in this field, in the framework of the Regional Episcopal Conference of West Africa, by creating a special commission to promote such a dialogue.

I know you are beginning to perceive the fruits of this mutually agreed upon decision; it gradually makes possible a real renewal of mentalities, which facilitates the beneficial transition from ignorance to knowledge of the Muslim faith, from indifference to opening, from rejection to dialogue.

Pope John Paul II, To the bishops of Senegal on their *ad limina* visit, Rome, 26 January 1982.

Spiritual richness of Islam

Christians and Muslims have many things in common, as believers and as human beings. We live in the same world, marked by many signs of hope, but also by multiple signs of anguish. For us, Abraham is a model of faith in God, of submission to his will and of confidence in his goodness. We believe in the same God, the one God, the living God, the God who created the world and brings his creatures to their perfection. ...

God asks that we should listen to his voice. He expects from us obedience to his holy will in a free consent of mind and heart. ...

It is he, God, who is our judge; he who alone is truly just. We know, however, that his mercy is inseparable from his justice. When man returns to him, repentant and contrite, after having strayed into the disorder of sin and the works of death, God then reveals himself as the one who pardons and shows mercy. To him, therefore, our love and our adoration! For his blessing and for his mercy, we thank him, at all times and in all places.

Man is a spiritual being. We believers know that we do not live in a closed world. We believe in God. We are worshippers of God. We are seekers of God.

The Catholic Church regards with respect and recognises the equality of your religious progress, the richness of your spiritual tradition. We Christians, also, are proud of our own religious tradition. I believe that we, Christians and Muslims, must recognise with joy the religious values that we have in common, and give thanks to God for them. Both of us believe in one God, the only God, who is all justice and all mercy; we believe in the importance of prayer, of fasting, of almsgiving, of repentance and of pardon; we believe that God will be a merciful judge to us all at the end of time, and we hope that after the resurrection he will be satisfied with us and we know that we will be satisfied with him.

Loyalty demands also that we should recognise and respect our differences. Obviously the most fundamental is the view that we hold on the person and work of Jesus of Nazareth. You know that, for Christians, Jesus causes them to enter into an intimate knowledge of the mystery of God and into a filial communion by his gifts, so that they recognise him and proclaim him Lord and saviour. These are important differences, which we can accept with humility and respect, in mutual tolerance; this is a mystery about which, I am certain, God will one day enlighten us.

Christians and Muslims, in general we have badly understood each other, and sometimes, in the past, we have opposed and often exhausted each other in polemics and in wars. I believe that today, God invites us to change our old practices. We must respect each other, and we must also stimulate each other in good works on the path of God.

With me, you know the reward of spiritual values. Ideologies and slogans cannot satisfy you nor can they solve the problems of your life. Only spiritual and moral values can do it, and they have God as their foundation.

Dear young people, I wish that you may be able to help in building a world where God may have first place in order to aid and to save mankind. On this path, you are assured of the esteem and the collaboration of your Catholic brothers and sisters whom I represent among you this evening.

Pope John Paul II, To young Muslims of Morocco, Casablanca, 19 August 1985.

Respect neighbour's creed

You must try to show your Muslim brethren and the followers of other religious traditions that your Christian faith, far from weakening your sense of pride in your homeland and your love for her, helps you to prize and respect the culture and heritage of Bangladesh. It inspires you to face the challenges of the present day with love and responsibility. The Catholic Church is committed to a path of dialogue and collaboration with the men and women of goodwill of every religious tradition. We have many spiritual resources in common which we must share with one another as we work for a more human world. Young people especially know how to be open with each other and they want a world in which all basic freedoms, including the freedom of religious belief, will be respected. Sometimes, Christians and Muslims fear and distrust one another as a result of past misunderstanding and conflict. This is also true in Bangladesh. Everyone, especially the young, must learn always to respect one another's religious beliefs and to defend freedom of religion, which is the right of every human being.

Pope John Paul II, To Christians (and others) in Bangladesh, 19 November 1986.

Dialogue on mission

The topic of your discussion is a timely one. Since we are believers in God - who is goodness and perfection - all our activities must reflect the holy and upright nature of the one whom we worship and seek to obey. For this reason, also in the works of mission and *da'wah* [summons], our actions must be founded upon a respect for the inalienable dignity and freedom of the human person created and loved by God. Both Christians and Muslims are called to defend the inviolable right of each individual to freedom of religious belief and practice. There have been in the past, and there continue to be in the present, unfortunate instances of misunderstanding, intolerance and conflict between Christians and Muslims, especially in circumstances where either Muslims or Christians are a minority or are guest workers in a given country. It is our challenge as religious leaders to find ways to overcome such difficulties in a spirit of justice, brotherhood and mutual respect. Hence, by considering the proper means of carrying out mission and *da'wah* you are dealing with an issue which is important both for religious and for social harmony.

You have also been addressing the difficulties faced today by those who believe in God in their efforts to proclaim his presence and his will for mankind. As believers, we do not deny or reject any of the real benefits which modern developments have brought, but we are convinced nevertheless that without reference to God modern society is unable to lead men and women to the goal for which they have been created. It is here too that Christians and Muslims can work together, bearing witness before modern civilisation to the divine presence and loving Providence which guide our steps. Together we can proclaim that he who has made us has called us to live in harmony and justice. May the blessing of the Most High accompany you in your endeavours on behalf of dialogue and peace.

Pope John Paul II, To the delegation of the World Islamic Call Society, Rome, 15 January 1990.

Readiness to work with Muslims

To all Muslims throughout the world, I wish to express the readiness of the Catholic Church to work together with you and all people of good will to aid the victims of the war and to build structures of a lasting peace not only in the Middle East, but everywhere. This cooperation in solidarity towards the most afflicted can form the concrete basis for a sincere, profound and constant dialogue between believing Catholics and believing Muslims, from which there can arise a strengthened mutual knowledge and trust, and the assurance that each one everywhere will be able to profess freely and authentically his or her own faith.

Injustice, oppression, aggression, greed, failure to forgive, desire for revenge, and unwillingness to enter into dialogue and negotiate: these are merely some of the factors which lead people to depart from the way in which God desires us to live on this planet. We must all learn to recognise these elements in our own lives and societies, and find ways to overcome them. Only when individuals and groups undertake this education for peace can we build a fraternal and united world, freed from war and violence.

I close my greeting to you with the words of one of my predecessors, Pope Gregory VII who in 1076 wrote to Al-Nasir, the Muslim Ruler of Bijaya, present day Algeria: 'Almighty God, who wishes that all should be saved and none lost, approves nothing in us so much as that after loving him one should love his fellow man, and that one should not do to others, what one does not want done to oneself. You and we owe this charity to ourselves especially because we believe in and confess one God, admittedly in a different way, and daily praise and venerate him, the creator of the world and ruler of this world.'

These words, written almost a thousand years ago, express my feelings to you today as you celebrate *'Id al-Fitr*, the Feast of the Breaking of the Fast. May the Most High God fill us all with his merciful love and peace.

Pope John Paul II, Message to the faithful of Islam at the end of the month of Ramadan, 3 April 1991.

Real efforts at understanding

As two religious communities who strive to submit ourselves without reserve to the will of God, we Christians and Muslims should live together in peace, friendship and cooperation. I am happy to note that, since the arrival of the first Christians in this land, the people of Senegal have given the world a good example of this sharing of life.

In May 1991, in a joint message to their fellow Christians, the Catholic bishops of Senegal, called attention to 'the real efforts at understanding and dialogue between Christians and Muslims, the meeting between religious leaders' which have been undertaken in your country. They noted that the young people have worked together to build cemeteries, mosques and churches; that school children engage in a healthy emulation to make their schools places of peace, forgiveness and fraternity; that adults work together to improve the life and community spirit of the country. I would like to support and encourage all these efforts at building a harmonious society because I am convinced that this is the way of God.

Our Creator and our final judge desires that we live together. Our God is a God of peace, who desires peace among those who live according to his commandments. Our God is the holy God who desires that those who call upon him live in ways that are holy and upright. He is a God of dialogue who has been engaged from the very beginning of history in a dialogue of salvation with the humanity which he created. This dialogue continues in the present day, and will go on until the end of time.

We Christians and Muslims must be people of dialogue. As I have often said, and as the bishops of Senegal have repeated, this commitment to dialogue means, first of all, 'a dialogue of life', a positive acceptance, interaction and cooperation by which we bear active witness, as believers, to the ideals to which God has called us.

Pope John Paul II, To Islamic leaders of Senegal, Dakar, 22 February 1992.

Points in common

I thank God who has often given me the opportunity of meeting Muslim religious leaders and the faithful of Islam during the course of my apostolic visits. No one should be surprised if brothers and sisters, believing in the one God, want to know one another better and share their experiences.

Many points common to Muslims and Christians are related to religious piety, such as the importance given to prayer, a regard for morality and a sense of the dignity of the human person open to the transcendent. There we recognise some sources of inalienable human rights. You understand why during his visit to the Catholic community of Benin the Pope, as head and pastor of the Church, could not fail to meet representatives of the Muslim communities.

In Benin, Christians and Muslims have been living side by side for a long time. I can only encourage the efforts of both sides to make progress in mutual knowledge and respect. Your country experienced times of glory and times of serious difficulty. The time has come when all Beninese, without distinction of tribe or religion, are called to join in the efforts for its reconstruction. The development of Benin, in which Muslims, Christians and members of the traditional religion must participate, should benefit all segments of the population, avoiding all forms of moral, physical or psychological violence. ...

Please, permit me to mention in turn another area in which Christians and Muslims can work hand in hand: the search for peace. 'The path of those who believe in God and desire to serve him is not that of domination. It is the way of peace: a union of peace with our Creator expressed in doing his will: peace within the whole created universe, by using its benefits wisely and for the good of all; peace within the human family, by working together to build strong bonds of justice, fraternity and harmony within our societies; peace in the hearts of all individuals' (Pope John Paul II, Message for the end of Ramadan, 1991).

Pope John Paul II, To representatives of the Muslims of Benin, Parakou, 4 February 1993.

True knowledge of others

Among your pastoral concerns, we must also note the Islamic revival, manifesting itself in the active presence of foreign preachers and sometimes involving violent aspects. Due to Islam's massive presence in Chad, and because of events in neighbouring countries, some Catholics are worried.

In such a difficult context as yours, and in view of the proselytising done by some Islamic activists promoting another kind of society, I invite you to maintain your training sessions on Islam. These sessions will help Christians rid themselves of prejudices engendered by ignorance. They will better discover the richness of their faith and be proud of it, and thanks to a solid foundation thus acquired, they will feel more secure in their dialogue with their Muslim brothers. I hope that wherever possible, while remaining vigilant regarding certain disloyal practices, 'the dialogue of life' between Christians and Muslims will continue and progress, as well as the 'dialogue of works of mercy.' One can also express the wish that volunteer work may contribute to greater solidarity and to sincere dialogue with the most open and generous of Muslims.

Pope John Paul II, To the bishops of Chad on their *ad limina* visit, Rome, 27 June 1994.

Fundamentalism

The subject you have chosen for your exchange is a sensitive one: fundamentalism in Islam and Christianity. Indeed, we notice such attitudes in various milieux; realising this you are able to proceed to an objective analysis of this phenomenon in Islam.

In the regions where you exercise your ministries, you have direct experience of the effects of Muslim fundamentalism which has expressed itself particularly these last few years. You need to take a certain distance and to remain level-headed to carry out your mission in this context. The phenomenon of fundamentalism must be studied in all its motivations and manifestations. The analysis of the political, social and economic situations shows that this phenomenon is not only religious but that, in many cases, religion is exploited for political purposes or else to offset social and economic difficulties. A lasting response to fundamentalism cannot be found until the problems that cause and nurture it are resolved. While intolerance and the violence fostered by fundamentalism must be condemned, it is of the utmost importance to look with faith and love upon the people who take these attitudes and who often suffer from them.

Your presence and your witness to Christ in Muslim countries are precious for the Church. I know that this is not without difficulty for you but I encourage you to go forth and bring the good news of the love of Christ our Saviour for all, he who said to his disciples: 'I am with you always; yes, to the end of time' (*Matthew* 28:20).

Pope John Paul II, To a Franciscan group involved in dialogue with Muslims, Castel Gandolfo, 26 August 1995.

Living with each other

It is important that Muslims and Christians continue to explore philosophical and theological questions together, in order to come to a more objective and comprehensive knowledge of each other's religious beliefs. Better mutual understanding will surely lead, at the practical level, to a new way of presenting our two religions not in opposition, as has happened too often in the past, but in partnership for the good of the human family.

Interreligious dialogue is most effective when it springs from the experience of 'living with each other' from day to day within the same community and culture. In Syria, Christians and Muslims have lived side by side for centuries, and a dialogue of life has gone on unceasingly. Every individual and every family knows moments of harmony, and other moments when dialogue broke down. The positive experiences must strengthen our communities in the hope of peace; and the negative experiences should not be allowed to undermine that hope. For all the time that Muslims and Christians have offended one another, we need to seek forgiveness from the Almighty and to offer each other forgiveness. Jesus teaches us that we must pardon others' offences if God is to pardon our own sins (cf. *Matthew* 6:14).

Pope John Paul II, Discourse during the visit to the Umayyad Mosque, Damascus, Syria, 6 May 2001.

5. Other faiths

Church becomes colloquium

Another matter that occupies your zeal is interreligious dialogue. This too is a serious part of your apostolic ministry. The Lord calls you, especially in the particular circumstances in which you are placed, to do everything possible to promote this dialogue according to the commitment of the Church. Paul VI dedicated a great part of his first encyclical to the subject of dialogue. He spelled out the need for dialogue, its conditions, its contents, its characteristics and its spirit. In describing dialogue, Paul VI stated: 'Before speaking, it is necessary to listen not only to a man's voice, but to his heart. ... The spirit of dialogue is friendship and, even more, is service' (*Ecclesiam Suam*, n. 87).

As bishops, you personify the loving Church of Christ that wishes to be open to the whole world, in order to listen and to offer friendship and service. The dialogue that you are called to is one of courteous respect, meekness and trust, from which all rivalry and polemics are excluded. It is a dialogue that springs from faith and is conducted in humble love. At the same time, 'the Church has something to say; the Church has a message to deliver; the Church has a communication to offer' (*Ecclesiam Suam*, n. 65). She truly wishes to speak about the transcendent destiny of man, about truth, justice, freedom, progress, harmony, peace and civilisation. This dialogue is of its nature directed towards collaboration on behalf of man and his spiritual and material wellbeing.

Pope John Paul II, To bishops of India, New Delhi, 1 February 1986.

Overcome religious intolerance

The question of human rights prompts us to note the signs of religious intolerance manifested in some Asian countries. Under the pressure of particular groups, for example, certain governments in nations where there are many followers of Islam have assumed postures which seem not in keeping with that tolerance which is part of the venerable Islamic tradition. Attempts are sometimes made to change legislation, introducing policies which effectively deny the rights of religious minorities. The intransigent attitudes of some, which leave no room for other religions, recognise as authentically Asian only that which can be expressed within their own religious categories. The regrettable phenomenon of intolerance is not, however, restricted to any single religious tradition.

Pope John Paul II, Letter to bishops of Asia, 23 June 1990.

Dialogue of collaboration

Especially since the Second Vatican Council, the Catholic Church has been fully committed to pursuing the path of dialogue and cooperation with the members of other religions. Interreligious dialogue is a precious means by which the followers of various religions discover shared points of contact in the spiritual life, while acknowledging the differences which exist among them. The Church respects the freedom of individuals to seek the truth and to embrace it according to the dictates of conscience. In this light she firmly rejects proselytism and the use of unethical means to gain conversions.

Pope John Paul II, To religious leaders of Sri Lanka, Colombo, 21 January 1995.

Irreversible commitment

Your efforts to uphold the spiritual values and to apply the light of the gospel to issues affecting the life of your nation are an immense service to the whole of Sri Lankan society. In the face of ethnic tensions and conflicts that affect your country and threaten human dignity and rights, you have a duty to speak out and encourage all men and women of goodwill to seek the triumph of justice, truth and harmony.

In your multireligious society, interreligious dialogue remains an important commitment for the Church at every level. Continue to 'build bridges' of understanding and cooperation with the followers of other religions, especially to promote respect for human life, concern for honesty and integrity in all areas of socio-economic and political life, and to work for the cause of peace and solidarity between individuals and social groups. In this way, too, the Church will bear effective witness to the kingdom of God and the truth of the gospel.

Pope John Paul II, To bishops of Sri Lanka, Colombo, 21 January 1995.

Eucharist, the source of dialogue

From the Eucharist comes strength to live the Christian life in all its fullness, and zeal to share that life with others. The Eucharistic Lord sends you into the highways and byways of your nation, to establish for God's glory 'the civilisation of love, founded on the universal values of peace, solidarity, justice and liberty, which find their full attainment in Christ' (*Tertio Millennio Adveniente*, n. 52). For bishops and their co-workers - priests, religious and committed lay persons - that task includes the teaching of the Church's social doctrine, the proclamation of the gospel of life, and the fostering of interreligious dialogue and cooperation.

In a multireligious society such as India, Christians need to join hands with other people of good will, in the defence of shared human and spiritual values and in the promotion of integral human development. The Catholic Church in India must meet the challenge of militant religious fundamentalism by fostering interreligious dialogue. From this dialogue will come respect for the 'seeds of the Word' sown among the peoples and religions of India, as well as a sincere recognition of the genuine 'spiritual riches' of their 'prayer and contemplation, faith and ways of searching for God or the Absolute' (*Evangelii Nuntiandi*, n. 42) The 'dialogue of life' with non-Christians will show that genuine religious belief is a source of mutual understanding, fraternal solidarity and social peace.

Pope John Paul II, To bishops of India on their *ad limina* visit, Rome, 13 December 1995.

Peace for religion

In some cases, Asian Christians dwell in lands scarred by conflicts, which are at times presented as the effect of religion. What a travesty of true belief this is! How unfaithful not only to the gospel but also to the great insights of the religions of Asia, which in their different ways teach tolerance and goodness. People of all religions must emphatically show that religion and peace go together!

But let there also be peace for religion. Let the right to freedom of belief and worship be respected in every part of this continent! For if this most basic of rights is denied, then the whole edifice of human dignity and freedom is shaken. *Ecclesia in Asia* clearly notes that in parts of Asia explicit proclamation is forbidden and religious freedom is denied or systematically restricted (n. 23). In such situations the Church bears witness through a 'taking up of her cross', all the while urging governments to recognise religious freedom as a fundamental human right.

Since Asia suffers greatly from the wound of division between Christians, the synod urges all Christ's followers to work ever harder to be 'of the same mind having the same love, being in full accord and of one mind' (*Philippians* 2:2) It likewise asks the whole Church in Asia to pour herself out in the *colloquium salutis*, the saving dialogue which reaches out to the followers of other religions and to all men and women of good will. In this dialogue, the word which we must speak is the word of the cross of Jesus Christ. For in him who emptied himself completely on the cross the fullness of life is found (cf. *Philippians* 2:6-11). The post-synodal apostolic exhortation *Ecclesia in Asia* invites the people of Asia to contemplate the figure of the crucified Jesus, who leads us through darkness to the door that opens on to the fullness of life which humanity seeks. With a special passion, Asia has always sought that fullness. We speak of a life which comes to us, not when the world's pain is averted or left behind, but when it is entered and transfigured by the power of self-emptying love, the love which is most clearly symbolised in the pierced heart of the Saviour on the cross. This is the love which makes Christian holiness possible. It gives rise to proclamation, to loving solidarity with those in need, to respect for and openness to every human being and to all peoples. Let no one fear the Church! Her one ambition is to continue Christ's mission of service and love, so that the light of Christ may shine more brightly, and the life that he gives may be more accessible to those who hear his call.

In presenting the fruit of the Synod's work, in the post-synodal apostolic exhortation *Ecclesia in Asia*, you the bishops, are being asked to make ever greater efforts to spread the gospel of salvation throughout the length and breadth of the human geography of Asia. The question is not whether the Church has something essential to say to the men and women of our time, but how she can say it clearly and convincingly (cf. n.29)! The Good Shepherd laid down his life for his sheep, and we who bear his name must follow the same path. With Saint Gregory of Nyssa we must pray for the strength to fulfil the ministry entrusted to us: 'Show me, Good Shepherd, where green pastures and restful waters lie; call me by my name, that I may hear your voice' (*Commentary on the Song of Songs*, n. 2). Successors of the Apostles, responsible for the body of Christ, shepherd the Church in Asia with loving care through every dark valley to green pastures and restful waters.

Pope John Paul II, To bishops of Asia, New Delhi, 6 November 1999.

Respect for religious liberty

I take this occasion to express my sincere interest in all the religions of India - an interest marked by genuine respect, by attention to what we have in common, by a desire to promote interreligious dialogue and fruitful collaboration between people of different faiths. In this regard, I note with admiration how the Indian constitution through its official recognition of religious liberty, honours the dignity of each person in his or her most sacred dimension, and at the same time allows the promotion of genuine spiritual values, which are so fundamental for social living.

Pope John Paul II, To the people of India, New Delhi, 1 February 1986.

Tribute to Gandhi

The figure of Mahatma Gandhi and the meaning of his life's work have penetrated the consciousness of humanity. In his famous words, Pundit Jawaharlal Nehru has expressed the conviction of the whole world: 'The light that shone in this country was no ordinary light'. ...

From this place, which is forever bound to the memory of this extraordinary man, I wish to express to the people of India and of the world my profound conviction that the peace and justice that this contemporary society has such great need of will be achieved only along the path which was at the core of his teaching: the supremacy of the spirit and *Satyagraha*, the 'truth-force' which conquers without violence by the dynamism intrinsic to just action.

The power of truth leads us to recognise with Mahatma Gandhi the dignity, equality and fraternal solidarity of all human beings, and it prompts us to reject every form of discrimination. It shows us once again the need for mutual understanding, acceptance and collaboration between religious groups in the pluralistic society of modern India and throughout the world.

Pope John Paul II, To the people of India at Raj Ghat, New Delhi, 1 February 1986.

Reconciliation between groups and individuals

In her outward service to a society in distress, the Church in your regions is called to realise her role in a multicultural, multireligious environment by joining hands with all people of good will in an honest interreligious dialogue, in an effort to raise the social and cultural levels and to improve the conditions of those in need. As the sacrament of the unity of the whole of the human family, the Church cannot but be an ardent promoter of human solidarity. She fosters attitudes of brotherhood and friendship. So many of her works and institutions are open to all.

In India, the Church has a special vocation to teach and foster reconciliation between individuals and groups, between people of different ethnic, social or cultural origins, She can do this only if she herself is a reconciled community, if her members reject in practice every form of discrimination and demonstrate in word and deed that they truly regard all men and women as brothers and sisters, children of the same Father and heirs to the same kingdom.

In a country like India where philosophy and religion are closely connected, priests and seminarians should be well trained in moral philosophy and medical ethics, so that they can take part in interreligious dialogue on questions related to the natural transmission of life and the value and inalienable dignity of every human life from the moment of conception to natural death.

Pope John Paul II, To bishops of India on their *ad limina* visit, Rome, 13 April 1989.

What we have in common

The Korean people throughout history have sought, in the great ethical and religious visions of Buddhism and Confucianism, the path to the renewal of self and to the consolidation of the whole people in virtue and in nobility of purpose. The profound reverence for life and nature, the quest for truth and harmony, self-abnegation and compassion, the ceaseless striving to transcend - these are among the noble hallmarks of your spiritual tradition that have led, and will continue to lead, the nation and the people through turbulent times to the haven of peace.

Our diversity in religious and ethical beliefs calls upon all of us to foster genuine fraternal dialogue and to give special consideration to what human beings have in common and to what promotes fellowship among them (*Nostra Aetate*, n. 1). Such concerted effort will certainly create a climate of peace in which justice and compassion can flourish.

Pope John Paul II, To the leaders of the various religions of Korea, Seoul, 6 May 1984.

Experience of Thai kindness

As the 'Upholder of All Religions' in Thailand, His Majesty the King has shown personal concern for the free practice of religions other than Buddhism in his country. For this reason I have been honoured by his invitation. …

My presence on Thai soil has also enabled me to greet His Holiness the Supreme Patriarch of all Buddhists in this country. It was a privilege for me to meet this venerable and revered religious leader. I am sure that our encounter augurs for the future of Buddhist-Catholic relations here and throughout the world.

Pope John Paul II, To various religious leaders of Korea, Bangkok, 11 May 1984.

Apex of love-compassion

Eight years ago I met with some of you, and with others when you accepted my invitation three years ago and we prayed together for peace in Assisi. I very well remember venerable Etai Yamada whom I met both in Tokyo and Assisi, and I admire the passionate desire for peace that led him this time also to head the Japanese delegation to Warsaw at the age of ninety-five. ...

Just as war comes to birth in the heart of man, so peace should be conceived in our heart. When I met the representatives of Japanese religions in Tokyo I quoted the words of the great Saicho: 'The apex of love-compassion is to forget oneself and serve others'. Christ's law too is summed up in the commandment of love: 'Love God with all your heart and your neighbour as yourself.' We religious men want to bear witness before the world to our respect and love for one another and our unceasing prayer for the peace of the world.

Pope John Paul II, To followers of various religions in Japan, Castel Gandolfo, 5 September 1989.

Search for interior peace

I am pleased to have this meeting with you, monks of the Christian and Buddhist traditions. I greet you Rimpoche, and the monks accompanying you on your peace pilgrimage, present here today with the Benedictine Abbot Primate and the members of the Commission for Monastic Interreligious Dialogue.

You were welcomed by Benedictine monks whose motto is precisely *pax* - peace. You have encouraged one another to promote this peace which our world so greatly needs. All human persons, conscious of the realities of today's world, must commit themselves to the cause of peace, through service, through negotiation. As monks, you use the means that are particular to you: prayer and the search for interior peace. As St Benedict says to his monks in the prologue to his Rule: 'Seek peace: pursue it'.

We experienced this truth in Assisi, on the occasion of the World Day of Prayer for Peace. If prayer is neglected, the whole edifice of peace is liable to crumble. Your dialogue at the monastic level is truly a religious experience, a meeting in the depth of the heart, animated by the spirit of poverty, mutual trust and profound respect for your own traditions. This experience cannot always be translated adequately into words, and often can best be expressed in prayer-filled silence.

Pope John Paul II, To Christian and Buddhist monks, Rome, 20 September 1989.

Build a civilisation of love

On a different plane, modern Japan offers many opportunities for a serious and fruitful interreligious dialogue with the followers of other religions, especially Shintoism and Buddhism. Catholics must be concerned to promote this dialogue, both because we all have a common origin as God's chosen creatures, and a common destiny in his eternal love, and because the Church's mission in the world is one of solicitude for the whole human family, especially in its search for truth, happiness and solidarity with all who suffer or are in want. Of vital importance is the dialogue of life between Catholics and the followers of other religious traditions, a dialogue which springs naturally from the presence of the Church's members in the social sphere, primarily in education, social works and communications. The laity in particular should be conscious of the importance of their witness and example in fostering understanding and cooperation among all people of goodwill. On your part, as pastors, there is need for further reflection on the difficult but vital questions raised by the inculturation of the faith. It is a question of continuing along the lines of what you have already taught in the booklet entitled *Guidelines for Catholics with Regard to Ancestors and the Dead*.

Perhaps interreligious dialogue is the proper context in which the Church in Japan can give attention to the widespread 'crisis of civilisation' which, as I wrote in *Tertio Millennio Adveniente*, is becoming more and more apparent in societies which are highly developed technologically but which are interiorly impoverished by the tendency to forget God or to keep him at a distance.

Pope John Paul II, To bishops of Japan on their *ad limina* visit, Rome, 25 February 1995.

Index of documents

**Pontifical Council for Interreligious Dialogue/
Secretariat for Non-Christians**

Congregation for the Doctrine of the Faith

Commission for Religious Relations with the Jews

International Theological Commission

RECENT PUBLICATIONS

The Search for Christian Unity

The Search for Christian Unity - approved by the Bishops' Conference of England and Wales - is a popular version of the Vatican's *Directory for the Application of Principles and Norms on Ecumenism.*

Chapter 1, 'The search for Christian unity', makes the Catholic Church's ecumenical commitment very clear.

Chapter 2, 'Organisation in the Catholic Church at the service of Christian unity', describes how the Church officially structures its search for unity.

Chapter 3, 'Ecumenical formation in the Catholic Church', deals with the vital issue of learning about ecumenism and forming an ecumenical attitude.

Chapter 4, 'Communion in life and spiritual activity among the baptised', spells out appropriate ways of sharing in prayer and in both sacramental and non-sacramental worship.

Chapter 5, 'Ecumenical co-operation, dialogue and common witness', looks at practical details of working, witnessing and sharing in dialogue together.

The Search for Christian Unity includes study questions and points for action, and a foreword by Cardinal Cormac Murphy-O'Connor.

The Search for Christian Unity, A5, 80 pages, £4.00, ISBN 0 905241 21 5.

RECENT PUBLICATIONS

Teachers of the Faith:
speeches and lectures by Catholic bishops

Six cardinals and three other bishops have contributed to a unique collection of speeches and lectures, entitled *Teachers of the Faith*. All of the lectures were delivered in Britain over the last 26 years, and have appeared in the pages of *Briefing*, the official monthly journal of the Catholic bishops of Britain.

- **Cardinal Basil Hume** speaks about his personal faith journey and Jesus Christ today.
- **Cardinal Thomas Winning** discusses the Church in the third millennium.
- **Cardinal Cahal Daly**'s two contributions concern Northern Ireland, and the moral challenges facing the Church.
- **Cardinal Joseph Ratzinger**'s address is on consumer materialism and Christian hope.
- **Cardinal Johannes Willebrands** asks, is Christianity anti-Semitic?
- **Archbishop Derek Worlock** reflects on Catholic education and the 1944 Education Act.
- **Bishop Alan Clark** discusses the movement to Christian unity.
- **Bishop James Sangu** of Tanzania examines justice in the African context.

The foreword is by Cardinal Cormac Murphy-O'Connor.

Teachers of the Faith: speeches and lectures by Catholic bishops, A5, 160 pages, £6.00, ISBN 0 905241 19 3

RECENT PUBLICATIONS

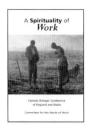

A Spirituality of Work

A Spirituality of Work, produced by the Committee for the World of Work of the Bishops' Conference of England and Wales, brings together prayers and Church teachings on work.

Chapter 1, 'Work in the sacred scriptures', examines the place of human work in God's plan since the beginning. Chapter 2, 'The Church's teaching on work', outlines the development of the Church's teaching on work, particularly as expressed in the Second Vatican Council and in the writings of the modern popes. Chapter 3, 'Human dignity and the value of work', explores this further, in the context of human dignity and the wider society. The fourth chapter provides prayers and meditations for individuals and for use in groups and church services, and a final section is a list of further Catholic resources.

A Spirituality of Work, A5, 52 pages, £2.50, ISBN 0 905241 18 5.

Briefing

Briefing is the official monthly journal of the Catholic Bishops' Conferences of Great Britain. It contains documents, information and news from the Church in Britain, Rome and overseas; official documents from the official sources.

£29.50 annual subscription.

Publications available from
Catholic Bishops' Conference of England and Wales
39 Eccleston Square   London SW1V 1BX